A Photographic Love Letter

to the Flora & Fauna of the Mojave Desert

Kollibri terre Sonnenblume

Macska Moksha Press
Portland, Oregon USA

Published in 2016 by Macska Moksha Press
9035 SE Washington Street
Portland, Oregon 97216
macskamoksha.com

Library of Congress Cataloging-in-Publication Data

Sonnenblume, Kollibri terre, 1969-

A Photographic Love Letter to the Flora & Fauna of the Mojave Desert / Kollibri terre Sonnenblume

ISBN: 978-0-9861881-6-9

1. Botany – General – Mojave Desert. 2. Zoology – General – Mojave Desert. I. Sonnenblume, Kollibri terre, 1969-. II. Title

Let me count the ways...

Though I was born and raised in the Midwest and have spent the majority of my adult life in Oregon (with a three year stint in Boston), I have a special, heartfelt love for the Mojave Desert. Compared to farm fields, lush forests or dense urban neighborhoods of those places, the desert is utterly exotic: the landscape of rugged mountains skirted with gently sloping alluvial flows amid flats of gravel or salt and dunes of sand; the vegetation, cacti -- smooth-skinned and spiny, shrubs -- hoary and grey-green, and flowers -- laughing with color in the spring; the animals, whether apparently prehistoric (the reptiles), seemingly out-of-place (the tortoise) or definitely adorable (the ground-squirrel), all gifted with marvelous adaptation for their harsh environment, each to their own.

I find all of it be sublime, which is to say, "of such excellence, grandeur, or beauty as to inspire great admiration or awe." I am not the first to feel that sentiment, nor, I am sure, the last.

I took all the pictures in this book during two visits to the area, from February to June in 2015 and from February through April in 2016. Photography has been a hobby of mine for over twenty years, since the last days of film, but I've never been as fascinated by my subjects as I was in the Mojave Desert. I had to purchase an external drive just to store all the resulting files. This collection was my attempt to showcase only the very best shots, although I admit I probably ended up picking some of my favorites instead.

Culturally, we think of the desert as being lifeless and empty, but that is hardly factual. The diversity of life, both flora and fauna, is vast, far more than most people realize or suspect, even among many who have been there. As a result, the area has not and does not get the respectful, caring touch it deserves and has suffered mightily from mining, ranching, military activity and urban encroachment. The newest threat is from large-scale renewable energy projects such as solar power plants and wind farms that threaten to wipe out large areas, including places that have managed to survive relatively intact until now.

And, of course, the people who knew best how to live in this tough-as-nails yet fragile environment, as life-affirming co-creating participants in the web of life -- the Native Americans -- were viciously driven to the margins by the European Conquest. It remains to be seen if they will ever be able to return home to show the rest of us a true meaning of the word, "sustainability." As the effects of Climate Change become more severe, their example, both material and spiritual, becomes more vital.

This book is only an introduction to its subject. Fortunately, there are many other resources out there for gaining appreciation of the Mojave Desert, including nature guides, memoirs, histories, novels, and works of art. Of course, a personal visit is the best way to know the area, and to fall in love oneself. My ultimate hope is that you will be inspired to take action to help defend this unique place. There are already people working on it, but they could use more help.

In the meantime, turn the page and enjoy!

Campin' out

During my 2016 visit, this 1986 Toyota pickup truck was my home. I slept out of the back and cooked my meals on a Coleman stove. I stayed in several different places but spent the most time at this particular spot in the Mojave National Preserve.

Those mountains are the Providence range, which reach an elevation of over 7000 feet (2100 m). This ecosystem is known as "Creosote Bush Scrub," named for its dominant plant, *Larrea tridentata*, which in Spanish is called, "Governadora," that is: a "governess," one who takes care of children. This is appropos since she acts as a nurse for smaller plants -- sheltering them from wind and sun -- and as a protector for small mammals, who dig tunnels amongst her roots to protect themselves from predators. Such mammals include the White-Tailed Antelope Ground Squirrel, White-Footed Mouse and Kangaroo Rat, featured later in this book.

Dune Primrose
(*Oenothera deltoides*)

Perennial herbaceaous plant in the Evening Primrose Family (Onagraceae) found in sandy places and disturbed areas. Also known as Devil's Lantern, Lion-in-a-Cage, Birdcage Evening Primrose, and Basket Evening Primrose. Flowers start out white and showy and fade to pink and raggedy. When the plant dries out at the end of its growing season, its branches curl up into a shape that resembles a lantern, cage or basket: hence the common names. This roundish form can break off at ground level and roll along the ground scattering seeds as it goes. This efficient means of self-dispersal makes the plant a common sight along roadsides.

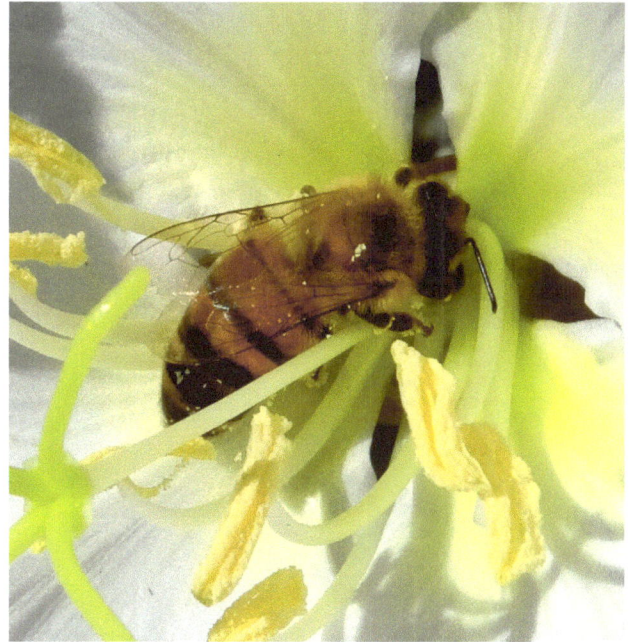

The flower's pollen is thread-like and sticky and cannot be easily collected by most bees, except for the Mining Bee, which has specially-shaped pollen bristles on its legs that make the job efficient. (Pictured above is a honey bee, digging in as deep as he can go.) The flower is a lurking spot for a yellow-green Crab Spider that hides among the anthers awaiting prey; it's coloration is so close to the flower's that it is nearly invisible.

Because the flower opens late in the day and stays open all night, it attracts the primarily nocturnal Sphinx moth, which is able to access the nectar deep down at the base of the flower with its long proboscis (a tongue-like, tube-shaped organ that sucks liquid). Pollen rubs off on the moth's legs and body as it feeds and is then transferred to the next flower it visits. The leaves and flowers are the primary food source of the moth's larvae.

The Cahuilla Native Americans harvested the Hawkmoth caterpillars for food when they were plentiful.

California Poppy
(*Eschscholzia* sp.)

At least a half dozen species of California Poppy grace the deserts of southern California, including *E. californica*, the state flower. Pictured above is *E. parishii* or *E. glyptosperma*, which are both more common in the Mojave. *E. minutiflora* is on the facing page, with an especially small specimen to the immediate right that illustrates why this one is known as "Pygmy Poppy."

"Eschscholzia" is named for Dr. Johann Friedrich Gustav von Eschscholtz (1753-1831), a Balkan surgeon, entomologist and botanist who visited California with the Russian expeditions of the early 1800's.

Desert Bluebells

(*Phacelia campanularia*)

Also known as Desert Bells, California Bluebell, Desert Canturbury Bells, Wild Canterbury Bells, Desert Scorpionweed, and Bluebell Phacelia. The first European to identify it was Charles Christopher Parry (1823-1890), an American naturalist, who sent seeds to England, where the plant is still popular in gardens. It's easy to see why!

Sacred Datura (*Datura wrightii*)

Also known as Thorn-Apple, Jimson Weed, Angel's Trumpet and Moonflower, this is a perennial herbaceous plant found in washes, roadsides and other disturbed areas. Large white trumpet-shaped blossoms open in the evening, stay open all night, and wilt in the morning. The flowers give off a sweet, narcotic odor, but the leaves smell (oddly) somewhat like peanut butter. All parts of the plant contain alkaloids responsible for its notorious mind-altering effects. Since these alkaloids can be deadly and their concentration varies from plant to plant, estimating an effective but non-lethal dosage is very tricky. Do not consume without guidance.

According to Daniel E. Moerman, author of Native American Ethnobotany, Datura is the "most universally used hallucinogenic and medicinal plant known to humans." Among the Cahuilla, says Moerman:

Datura offered the shaman not only a means to transcend reality and come into contact with specific guardian spirits, it also enabled him to go on magical flights to other worlds or transform himself into other life forms such as the mountain lion or eagle. Such magical flights were a necessary and routine activity for Cahuilla shaman [who] might use the drug to visit the land of the dead, returning to the profane world with information useful to his people, or he might pursue a falling star to recapture a lost soul and return it to its owner.

Greater Roadrunner
(*Geococcyx californianus*)

Also known as Ground Cuckoo, Chaparral Cock, Snake Killer and, in Mexican Spanish, *Paisano*. This bird was the model for the famous cartoons from Warner Bros. featuring a bumbling coyote as the roadrunner's eternal nemesis. In real life, coyotes can outrun roadrunners.

Roadrunners are unable to fly for long distances and mostly travel on the ground, often moving quickly as they hunt. They can run at 20 mph (32 km/h) with reported sprints of up to 26 mph (42 km/h). Their diet consists of insects, spiders, scorpions, small mammals and snake. They are especially fond of lizards, and baby roadrunners are fed little else.

Roadrunners are creatures of habit, often with a daily route that they follow punctually. Around humans they are often not shy and can even be playful. The particular specimen in these photographs was a regular, though not daily, visitor to my friend's home in the town of Joshua Tree. He seemed happy to pose for the camera, giving me the great shot on the facing page.

Beavertail Cactus

(*Opuntia basilaris* var. *basilaris*)

The pads, buds, flowers, fruits and seeds are edible and were a staple food of the Cahuilla. They rolled the pads in sand to remove the spines and baked them in stone-lined pits. Buds were dried and stored. The Kumeyaay, Kawaiisu and Tübatulabal also ate this plant. The Shoshone treated wounds and the accompanying pain with a poultice of the pulp and rubbed the fuzz-like spines into warts and moles to remove them.

All parts of the plant are eaten by the Desert Tortoise. The fruits and seeds are eaten by the White-Tailed Antelope Ground Squirrel, Rock Squirrel, Ring-tailed Cat and occasionally the Coyote. The pads are an important source of water for the Desert Woodrat. Beavertail Cactus exudes nectar from dots on its pads and flower buds that attract ants which not only collect the nectar for them- selves but also prey upon other insects that are potentially harmful.

Diamond Cholla (*Cylindropuntia ramosissima*)

Also known as Pencil Cactus, Pencil Joint Cactus and Darning Needle Cactus. "Diamond" describes the pattern of sections on the flesh. Skin color varies from green to purple. Flowers range from green or yellow to brown or red. The Cahuilla ate the fruit fresh, the stalks in soup and dried both for storage.

"Cylindro" is Greek for "round," and "opuntia" is an old Latin name used by Pliny, the Roman writer, and is derived from "Opus," a city where a cactus-like plant grew; "ramosissima" is Latin for "very much branched," which this dense plant most definitely is!

Silver Cholla (*Cylindropuntia echinocarpa*)

Cactus Wrens make nests among the prickly branches, protected by the spines from their predators. The Desert Woodrat eats the flesh without injury and incorporates the easily detached joints into the fortifications around its den. The Cocopa, Maricopa and Mojave Native Americans rolled the fruits in sand to remove the spines and ate them raw, while the Yavapai boiled them. The Tohono O'odham baked the buds and joints.

Following pages:
Mojave Prickly Pear
(*Opuntia phaeacantha*)
Strawberry Hedgehog Cactus
(*Echinocereus engelmannii*)

White-Tailed Antelope Ground Squirrel
(*Ammospermophilus leucurus*)

While living in the village of Joshua Tree in the Spring of 2015, my friend Clara and I met a delightful animal whose scientific name, *Ammospermophilus leucurus*, literally translates as "white-tailed sand and seed lover." One individual in particular started hanging out nearby when we came outside in the morning. She was plumpish and matronly, and sported a shorter-than-usual tail from an injury, so we named her "Mrs. Stubbs" (pictured on facing page).

We tossed out sunflower seeds for her which she would busily shell and stuff in her cheeks. Before long, she was eating out of our hands. Before much longer, others were showing up and a daily ritual was born.

In "Our Desert Neighbors," biologist Edmund C. Jaeger, writes:

The antelope "chipmunk," that vivacious animal midget that literally bounces over the ground, carrying his small, flattened, white-backed tail jauntily curled over his back, is the gayest little mammal of the desert. Sprightly, restless, and seemingly always possessed of the vigorous spontaneity of youth, he is among the favorites of all who know him. Especially are you fortunate if you have this chipper little rodent take up living quarters in the neighborhood of your desert home, for then you may watch him in all his sportive moods and know his engaging family life at firsthand.

We did indeed consider ourselves "fortunate" that these charming animals were part of our daily routine and we learned a lot about them by watching them at such close-quarters. When feeding in groups, they were highly competitive, constantly jockeying for position, vocalizing adverbly and chasing each other off.

But when danger was near, they were all-for-one and one-for-all. Approaching threats were announced by a loud, almost bird-like chittering. Then they would scatter, some taking cover under shrubs or in their burrows, others ascending to higher points to keep an eye out. The alarm would be taken up at other spots in the surrounding desert. After the danger had passed, they would return to their foraging and squabbling as if nothing had happened.

We enjoyed their company every day for weeks. When we left, I missed our friends for months afterwards. I still enjoy the memory of those jovial souls.

Mojave Yucca

(*Yucca schidigera*)

Also known as "Spanish Dagger" for its sharp, pointy leaves. Most common Yucca of the North American deserts, especially in southern California. Grows to a height of 8-12 feet (2.6-4 m). Superficially resembles the Joshua Tree to people who are new to the area, but the Joshua Tree is generally branchier, grows taller and has much shorter leaves.

The Cahuilla, Hualapai, Luiseño, and Mojave were among the tribes that ate the flowers and fruits in a variety of preparations, raw, cooked, and ground into meal. This plant provided fibers that could be used for many purposes: the Cahuilla made baskets, bowstrings, netting, strings, and brushes for body painting. The Kumeyaay and Hualapai made sandals and other Southwest Native Americans made cordage to use as a base for fur garments. The roots contain saponins, a detergent-like substance that makes suds when agitated in water. Various tribes bathed themselves in this water for cleanliness and for ceremony. Medicinally, it was used to treat dandruff, hair loss, headaches, bleeding, gonorrhea, arthritis and rheumatism.

The fruit's bitter outer coating, which is high in sugar, is eaten by the Desert Woodrat. Fruits and seeds are eaten by birds and small mammals, including the White-Tailed Antelope Ground Squirrel. Plant's height makes it a good roost for birds. Fallen branches and trunks provide critical habitat for the Desert Night Lizard, which waits out the hot days in their shade. Flwoers are pollinated by the "Yuccasella" Yucca Moth, whose larvae eat the developing seeds. New shoots are larval food of the Colorado Yucca Borer butterfly, an activty that can assist in the plant's clonal reproduction: when eating, the caterpillars often sever the underground rhizome connecting the mother and child plants, which then become independent.

Brown-Eyed Primrose

(*Chylismia claviformis*)

One of my very favorites, but the Mining Bee
expresses an even stronger preference, collecting
pollen only from this plant, mating among the
flowers, and nesting in sandy places close by.
Maybe I can come back as one!

Scorpionweeds
(*Phacelia* sp.)

Over 60 species of *Phacelia* are native to the Mohave Desert. A few, like the ones featured here, are quite common. "Phacelia" is Greek for "a cluster," which refers to the crowded flowers in many species of this genus.

"Bee's Friend" is another name for Lacy Phacelia *(P. tanacetifolia)*, which is used in agriculture to attract pollinating insects and as a covercrop. Gardeners plant it as an ornamental in the US and Europe. The leaves are edible but rarely consumed.

Facing page:
Distant Phacelia (*P. distans*)

This page, clockwise from top right:
Calthaleaf Phacelia (*P. calthafolia*)
unknown Phacelia with Honey Bee
Cleftleaf Wildheliotrope (*P. crenulata*)

Scale Bud

(*Anisocoma acaulis*)

Annual in the Sunflower Family (Asteraceae), which grows in sandy soils. "Anisocoma" is Greek for "unequal tufts of hair," which describes the differing lengths of the bristles in the flower's pappus, that is, the in bunch of fuzzy bits that form when it's going to seed, as seen below. "Acaulis" is Latin for "stemless" and apparently refers to the lack of stems on the leaves, which make a rosette at ground level. This is a fair weather flower that opens only in sunshine and closes in the shade or on a cloudy day.

Carpenter bees, genus *Xylocopa*

Above and below:
Bee Fly, genus *Systoechus*

Bees

Where there are flowers, there are pollinators, and bees were the most common ones I saw on my journeys. One day I even witnessed a swarm, which flew through my camp on its way to start a new hive.

Above and right:
Mining Bee, genus *Andrena*

Facing page:
Honey Bee, genus *Apis*

Bigelow's Monkeyflower
(*Mimulus bigelovii*)

Above:
Freckled Milk Vetch, aka Rattle Pod
(*Astragalus lentiginosus*)

Following pages:
California Cleome (*Peritoma arborea*)
Catsclaw Acacia (*Senegalia gregii*)

Lupines

There are dozens of species and sub-species in the genus *Lupinus* in southern California. Identifying an individual plant is a challenge, even if you're trained in botany. You end up investigating the shapes of the flowers, leaves and seeds, the relative lengths of stems, the degree of fuzziness, etc., seeking differences that can be minute.

One species unmistably distinguishes itself, however: *Lupinus excubitus*, named "Grape Soda Lupine," because the scent of the flowers is just like grape soda. No kidding! What are the chances? It is pictured on the right, but you'll have to take my word for it since it was impractical to include a scratch-n-sniff card with this book. ☺

"Lupinus" is Latin for "wolf," because it was falsely believed that Lupines rob the soil of fertility. In fact, like many species in the Legume Family, it captures nitrogen from the air and enriches poor soils. "Excubitus," is from the Latin verb, "to watch over," and refers to its tall, upright growth habit. So another common name for this species could be "Watchful Wolf."

Apricot Mallow
(*Sphaeralcea ambigua*)

Botanist Edmund C. Jaeger described this plant as "so handsome when in flower that many desert folk think it the climax of floral beauty." Indeed! This plant quickly became one of my favorites. It dotted the landscape around the town of Joshua Tree, an occasional but showy splash of color.

But I had my mind blown in May while driving through the Mojave National Preserve. There, its blooming spikes filled the flats for acres and acres. Astounded, I pulled over. It was a sight so startlingly beautiful that it took away not only my breath but also my sense of self. For a moment, there was no "I." There was only the vision.

Of course a photograph doesn't convey all that, but here's one anyway.

California Patch (*Chlosyne californica*)

Butterflies & Moths!

At least 75 species of butterflies and many more moths can be found in the Mojave Desert. Larvae tend to have narrow preferences for food sources, depending on just one or a handful of plants. Adults are less choosy when it comes to nectar sources. The Joshua Tree and Mojave Yucca are entirely dependent on one species of moth for pollination of their flowers. Native Americans used to eat the caterpillars of the White-Lined Sphinx Moth when they were plentiful.

Above: Owlet Moth (*Heliolonche pictipennis*)

Below: Larva of White-Lined Sphinx (*Hyles lineata*)

Following pages:
Western Tailed Blue (*Satyrium sylvinus*)
Flower Moth (*Schinia ligeae*)

Above: Purple Mat (*Nama demissum*)

Facing page:
Froebel's Four O'Clock (*Mirabilis multiflora*)

Following pages:
White Tidy Tips (*Layia glandulosa*)
Desert Indian Paintbrush (*Castelleja angustifolia*)

Phlox Family
(Polemoniaceae)

Phlox is a plant family found almost exclusively in North and South America, with the highest concentration of species in California. Among its distinguishing characteristics are flowers that have five petals, five sepals (the flaps on the bud that separate as it opens) that are fused at their common base, and five stamens (the male parts of the flower, which produces pollen). Pollen can be white, yellow, blue, or red. All of the species of Phlox that I encountered in the Mojave Desert were annuals of small size, many of them easy to miss.

Facing page: Humble Gilia (*Linanthus demissus*)

This page, clockwise from top right:
Golden Gilia (*Leptosiphon aureus*)
Broadleaf Gilia (*Aliciella latifolia*)
Unidentified species in *Gilia* genus

Above: Lilac Sunbonnet (*Langloisia setosissima* ssp. *punctata*), as observed in the Mojave National Preserve

Phlox Family *(from previous page)*

Facing page, clockwise from top left:
Lilac Sunbonnet, in Death Valley
Blue Mantle (*Eriastrum densifolium*)
Desert Woollystar (*Eriastrum eremicum*)

Chuckwalla (*Sauromalus ater*)

This lizard might look intimidating but is not a predator, surviving on a diet of flowers, leaves and fruit. Juvenile lizards occasionally eat insects, but not after their first year. When threatened, Chuckwallas wedge themselves in rock crevasses by puffing up their bodies. They are harmless to humans, though the converse is not true; they are captured for pets and their habitat is degraded by ranching and development. The scientific name means, "dark, flat lizard." "Chuckwalla," comes from the Cahuilla word, "caxwal," which was adapted from the Shoshone, "tcaxxwal."

Common Side-Blotched Lizard (*Uta stansburiana*)

This common lizard grows up to 2.5 in (6 cm) long, plus tail. Males are divided into three distinct "morphs," marked by throat color, either orange, yellow or blue. The different morphs utilize their own competitive mating strategies that trump one another through a "rock-scissors-paper" mechanism that results in seasonal changes in the number of any given morph. Oranges are "ultradominant" and keep harems, blues are merely "dominant" and monogamous, while yellows are "sneakers" who mate with unguarded females belonging to the others and can disguise themselves by mimicking females. Oranges have the highest mortality rates and yellows the highest fertility. Blues are better than oranges at catching yellows.

Desert Iguana
(*Dipsosaurus dorsalis*)

Mostly herbivorous, with a special fondness for the flowers of the Creosote Bush. Can grow to 2 feet (60 cm) in length, including tail, which is up to 1 1/2 times longer than its body. Territorial only during mating season.

Desert Spiny Lizard
(*Sceloporus magister*)

Diet is mostly carnivorous, including smaller lizards. Adults can be as long as 6.5 inches (16.5 cm), plus tail. Like other lizards, often does "push-ups" as display to defend territory. Belly can be bright blue! Often found near Joshua Trees and Mojave Yuccas.

Desert Night Lizard

(*Xantusia vigilis*)

Pictured here is a juvenile, but adults only grow to a length of 1.5 to 2.75 in (3.8 to 7.0 cm), plus tail. In a habit that's unusual for reptiles, they form social units that include parents and children. They often live around yuccas, including Joshua Trees.

Southern Desert Horned Lizard

(*Phrynosoma platyrhinos*)

Sometimes called "Horny Toads," this striking creature can be found from Idaho to northern Mexico. The subspecies in the Mojave Desert is called *calidiarum*, which means "hot" and describes the climate. Its diet is mostly insects and they will cover themselves partly in sand to hide while waiting for prey. They are shy around humans and will generally hide under a bush if approached. I spent ten minutes with this one as it worked its way across my campsite.

Desert Dandelion
(*Malacothrix glabrata*)

One of the best known wildflowers in the Mojave Desert because it loves to grow along roadsides. A thoroughly cheerful plant!

Facing page:

Orange Glandweed
(*Adenophyllum cooperi*)

Also known as "Dyssodia," which is Greek for an "unpleasant smell," this plant releases a strong scent when touched.

Desert Fivespot

(*Eremalche rotundifolia*)

Love at first sight. That's how it was for me with this flower. I was in Death Valley during the 2016 Spring bloom, on a botanizing weekend put on by the California Native Plant Society. We found these on the side of the road, in gravelly soil. I'm a sucker for Malvaceae (the Mallow Family) anyway, but I was instantly taken by this plant's charms: its rose-like buds with scarlet-margins, its degrees of opening from globe to cup by way of an expanding oculus, its stage make-up of five red spots, and its pink-pollened stamens ringed around the female pistil like orderly suitors. It even has heart-shaped leaves.

Desert Hyacinth

(*Dichelostemma capitatum*)

Also known as Purplehead, Wild Hyacinth, Blue Dicks, Covena, Papagolily and Brodiaea. The plant sends up shoots of long, grass-like leaves from "corms," which are enlarged, fleshy portions of the stem that grow underground, much like bulbs. Corms produce "cormlets" that become new plants. Corms and cormlets can go dormant for years at a time if they are too shaded by other vegetation and then re-sprout after a fire has cleared the area.

Many Native American tribes throughout this plant's range harvested the corms as an important food source and kept patches productive by replanting corms and cormlets, sowing seeds, and setting controlled burns. Early European settlers, copying Native Americans, ate the corms and called them "Grass Nuts."

Desert Hyacinth is an example of a plant that once benefited from its relationship with humans, who propagated it widely. The interruption of these activities (along with ranching and agriculture) has decreased its population. Unfortunately, most conservationists oppose the resumption of such relationships under the misguided notion that nature can only be protected with a strict hands-off policy. If asked, the Desert Hyacinth might very well voice a different opinion.

Golden Suncup
(*Chylismia brevipes*)

Threadleaf Groundsel
(*Senecio flaccisus*)

Mojave Buckwheat

(*Eriogonum fasciculatum*)

A common perennial flower found in many habitats. The seeds are edible and various Native Americans ate them in season and stored them for winter use as well as applying them medicinally. The Coahuila used them for headaches, stomach pain and as an eyewash, the Ohlone for urinary problems, and the Kumeyaay as a heart tonic, an emetic (vomit inducer), and for babies with diarrhea. The Zuni made a poultice of the powdered root for healing wounds and a root tea for sore throats and to heal lacerations suffered during childbirth. The Kawaiisu pierced their ears with the wood and lined acorn granaries with the leaves to keep the harvest dry.

The specific epithet, "fasciculatum," is Latin for "bundle" because the leaves grow from the stems in bunches that are called "fascicles."

Also known as "California Buckwheat," this plant is an important nectar source for bees, including the Honey Bee. Butterflies also feed on the flowers including the Mormon Metalmark, Behr's Metalmark, Gorgon Copper, Bramble Hairstreak, Bernardino Dotted-Blue, Boisduval's Blue, and the endangered El Segundo Blue. Larvae of Behr's Metalmark butterfly eat the leaves and hibernate in the dead flower heads. The seeds are scavenged by small mammals such as the Western Harvest Mouse.

White-Footed Mouse
(*Peromyscus leucopus*)

I did not meet this creature under the best of circumstances. While camped out, I ended up moving my truck every few days as the wind shifted so the opened back-end would be sheltered. One morning after doing this I found a dead mouse on the ground, cut cleanly in half, where the front end of my truck had been. At first I was mystified, but soon I made a guess and popped open the hood. Sure enough, the sliced up body parts of a few more mice were stuck to various places in the engine and frame. Apparently, a group of them had made a home in the fan and were killed when I started the engine. There were at least four mice total, by tail count. I collected all the remains I could find and gave them a decent burial, which included a tobacco offering and an apology.

A few hours later, this little guy showed up, stopped at the spot that would've been below his former home, and sat there in the bright sun, looking at me. This animal is nocturnal, so stationing himself in the open during the day was very unusual behavior. I looked back at him, opened my mind, and immediately felt his sadness. He was not full grown and that had been his family. I felt like a general who has just bombed a city, how being approached by an orphaned child making an appeal.

After a few moments of reflection, I scooped him up and put him in a cardboard box half full of fabric scraps which I set in the back of the truck with me. He squeaked when I touched him but soon made himself at home, nestling down into the fabric and falling asleep. From time to time during the day, I peeked in to check on him. If my movement disturbed him, he would open his eyes halfway and glare, but otherwise he continued to doze away.

He woke up around sunset and ate some sunflower seeds. I did not want to take him on as a pet unless it felt as though that's what he was demanding of me, so I set him up so his own choice would be clear to me. I put the box outside, out of the wind, angled so he could hop in and out on his own, and went to bed myself.

In the morning he was gone, and I didn't see him again, so I could only conclude that he had found a new home for himself, but whether that was in a burrow near or far or in the belly of a predator, I had no way of knowing. I also remained mystified about why he had approached me in the first place but was grateful that, it seemed, I was able to offer him some kind of comfort during his experience of loss. I guess I can't hope for much more for myself.

Joshua Tree (*Yucca brevifolia*)

Also known as Tree Yucca, Yucca Palm, Palm Tree Yucca, and *Izote de Desierto* (Desert Dagger). The Cahuilla Native Americans called it *Hunuvat chiy'a* and *Humwichawa* (which I like the best, of all the names). Mormon settlers named it after Joshua, a character in the Bible who was famous for raising his arms skyward in prayer. It can grow to be 49 feet (15 m) tall – 20-30 feet (9-13 m) on average – with root systems that extend 36 feet (11 m) away from the base. Age is difficult to determine because it lacks growth rings but estimates based on other means suggest potential lifespans in the centuries.

Native Americans used most of plant's parts: The Cahuilla ate the flowers, the Tübatulabal the immature pods, and the Kawaiisu the pits of the fruit, which they roasted, mashed, dried and stored. The Cahuilla made sandals and nets from the fibers,

(continued on next page)

(from previous page)

while the Kawaiisu, Shoshone and Timbisha used the red inner roots in basket-making.

The Joshua Tree is central to its ecosystem and plays roles for many desert animals. It is a nesting location for at least 25 species of birds and owls, hunting grounds and shelter for lizards, a high vantage point for ground squirrels, a source of housing material for the Desert Woodrat, and home and mating territory for dozens of species of insects. Fruits are eaten by the White-Tailed Antelope Ground Squirrel and the Mojave Ground Squirrel, who will both climb up to the tops of the trees to harvest them.

The trunk is a favorite drilling site for the Ladder-Backed Woodpecker. Fallen branches and trunks provide critical habitat for the Desert Night Lizard, which waits out the hot days in their shade. New shoots are larval food of the Colorado Yucca Borer butterfly. In the Pleistocene Era, over 10,000 years ago, the seeds might have been dispersed in part by the Shasta Ground Sloth; they have been found in the sloth's ancient dung heaps in dry caves.

In a classic case of what biologists call a "mutualistic relationship," the flowers are pollinated exclusively by two species of Yucca Moth and the diet of their larvae is comprised entirely of the Joshua Tree's developing seeds. When it is egg-laying time, the female moth uses tentacle-like mouth parts to collect pollen, which she forms into a clump and stores in hairs under her chin. (She is specially equipped with these parts instead of the tongue-like proboscis that moths and butterflies typically have.)

She then flies to a different flower on a different tree (which happens to ensure genetic diversity) and – using olfactory organs on her antennae – checks by smell to see if the flower has already been pollinated by another moth. If there's vacancy, she pierces the base of the flower's ovary with her sharply pointed ovipositor ("egg-placer") and lays eggs inside one of the ovary's six chambers.

Last, she takes some of the pollen from under her chin and places it on the end of the stigma, the flower's female part

that tops the ovary. In this way, the flower is pollinated and when the larvae hatch, they will have food on-hand in the form of the developing seeds. Generally, the larvae don't eat all the seeds, leaving behind enough for new plants. The tree can take care of itself, though: too many eggs in one flower will cause the ovary to abort its seeds, starving the moth larvae.

I'm not a Creationist, but it's difficult for me to imagine how such a complex (and frankly wonderous) relationship is purely the result of random mutations.

Wishbone Four O'Clock (*Mirabilis laevis*)

"Mirabilis" is Latin for "marvelous," which is apt for this lovely creation. "Wishbone" describes the shapes of the branches. Flowers open late in the afternoon (as the name suggests) and wilt right away if picked. Among Native Americans, the Luiseño drank a tea of the leaves as a purgative and the Mahuna used it for fevers. It is also a larval food plant for the White-Lined Sphinx moth.

Facing page:
Clavate-Fruited Primrose
(*Chylismia claviformis
ssp. lancifolia*)

Rambling Milkweed   (*Sarcostemma hirtellum*)

Coyote Tobacco *(Nicotiana obtusifolia)*

This plant was smoked ceremonially or for pleasure by many Native Americans. Some tribes, including the Quechan and Havasupai, encouraged its growth by burning the wood of Mesquite and scattering seeds in the cool ashes. The Paiute tribe mixed Coyote Tobacco with Mistletoe and smoked it out of pipes made from the swollen stems of Desert Trumpet *(Eriogonum inflatum)*. Ethnobotanist Daniel Moerman describes its role for the Cahuilla as "an integral part of every ritual. Used by shamans to control rain, increase crop production, divining and... at community gatherings, to drive away malevolent powers... Leaves smoked by travelers to clear away all danger and ensure blessing from spiritual guides."

Beetles

Clockwise from top left:
Ladybird Beetles (in the family Coccinellidae)
Ornate Checkered Beetle (*Trichodes ornatus*)
Blister Beetle (*Eupompha elegans*)
Beetle in the genus *Nemognatha*

Clockwise from top left:
Wood-boring Beetle (*Acmaeodera* sp.)
Morrison's Blister Beetle (*Lytta morrisoni*)
Three-Lined Potato Beetle (*Lema daturaphila*)

Burroweed Strangler

(*Orobanche cooperi*)

A member of the Broomrape Family, this parasitic plant entirely lacks chlorophyll and survives by leeching nutrients from other plants by boring into their roots with its own.

Facing page:
White Ratany
why not "Dragon Flower"?
(*Krameria bicolor*)

The "Belly Plants" of the Pebble Plains

A tiny geological treasure can be found in the San Bernadino Mountains of southern California: the "Pebble Plains." Located near the famous ski town of Big Bear Lake, this 92 square-mile area exhibits a soil type found nowhere else in the world, a combination of clay and quartz fragments left behind by a glacier lake that existed during the Pleistocene Era. Over the last 10,000 years, these ingredients have been subject to repeated swelling and shrinking from the freezes at that altitude (6000-7500 feet) and the sun's heat at that latitude (34° North), resulting in a unique composition.

Tiny botanical treasures are also found there. They are colloquially called "Belly Plants" because they are so small you have to get down on your belly to see them. About a dozen of the species there are found nowhere else in the world, having evolved in isolation, adapting to the unique soil.

Like all other ecosystems worldwide, this one is at risk from the effects of Climate Change. According to the Big Bear (California) Grizzly newspaper, "lower-than-average snow pack [in 2013] reduced water levels in the pebble plains clay and caused problems for several of the plant species." The water situation worsened during the following two years; snow packs and winter precipitation in 2015 were at all-time lows in California.

The Pebble Plains are within the San Bernadino National Forest and a portion of them are protected within the boundaries of the Baldwin Lake Ecological Reserve. The Reserve features a half-mile loop trail where you can see many Belly Plants. Admission is free-of-charge. Some of the same plants can also be found at nearby Doble Trail Camp, which is just steps off of the Pacific Crest Trail.

April through June is blooming season for most of the Belly Plant species. I visited with Clara in the Spring of 2015, and again by myself in 2016 and was thrilled by what I saw.

Siver-haired Ivesia
(*Ivesia argyrocoma* var. *argyrocoma*)

Southern Mountain Phlox (*Phlox austromontana*)

Facing page: Rayless Fleabane
(*Erigeron aphanactis* var. *congestus*)

Above: Parish's Rockcress (*Boechera parishii*)

Below: Pursh's milkvetch (*Astragalus purshii*)

Above: Alkali draba (*Cusickiella dougasii*)

Below: Slender Phlox (*Microsteris gracilis*)

Above: Slender Popcorn Flower
(*Plagiobothrys tenellus*)

Above: Small-fowered Collinsia (*Collinsia parviflora*)

Below: Golden Violet (*Viola dougasii*)

California Fan Palm
(*Washingtonia filifera*)

A relic species, left over from a time when the Mojave Desert was a tropical forest with plentiful rainfall. Fossil records show that it was widespread in the area ten million years ago. Now it is only found by streams, springs and in oases, such as the one pictured here, "Forty-Nine Palms," in Joshua Tree National Park.

Annually, each tree puts out up to ten stalks that can each produce 40 pounds (18 kilograms) of fruit so in a good year (read "wet"), a harvest of 400 pounds (180 kilograms) per tree is possible. California Fan Palm is threatened by agricultural and urban water projects that draw down water tables.

The genus, "Washingtonia," is inexplicably named for George Washington, who never saw one of these trees; "filifera" is Latin for "thread-bearing," and refers to the leaf edges.

California Fan Palms are animal magnets. Cactus Wrens find shelter in the "skirt" of old leaves on the trunks. Arizona Hooded Orioles and Scott's Orioles construct their nests from the leaf threads. California Treefrogs sing in it, Western Yellow Bats roost in it and Red-Spotted Toads breed in the water beneath it. Coyotes help distribute the seed in their scat. Flowers are eaten by larvae of the appropriately named Palm Flower Moth. The grubs of the Giant Palm Borer beetle make tunnels through the trunks, eating as they go, and can eventually kill older trees.

The Cahuilla Native Americans set up villages in oases and planted the tree throughout its natural range. They harvested the fruit by hooking the stalks with long, notched branches cut from Desert-Willows. Besides eating straight from the tree, they made jelly, soaked the fruit in water to brew a beverage, and ground the seeds into flour for porridge.

The tree was also a source of crafts. They used the fronds to flail seed pods and to wind- and waterproof living structures, the branches to fashion cooking utensils and bows, and the leaves to make hoops for children's toys. Ceremonially, they made images of the dead out of the leaves and burned them as part of memorial rites. The leaves and fibers were well-suited for basketry and clothing.

Amargosa toad
(*Anaxyrus nelsoni*)

I felt quite fortunate to meet this rare amphibian since it can only be found in a limited area: a 10 mile (16 km) stretch of the Amargosa River and nearby springs in Nye County, Nevada. They grow to be 3-5 inches (7.5-12.75 cm) long, with females generally larger than the males, and can live up to 12 years. Their habitat is threatened by factors including water diversion for development and flood control, off-road vehicles, cattle and non-native predators. Local efforts are being made to protect it, with some success.

Desert Tortoise
(*Gopherus agassizii*)

Like the California Fan Palm, this animal is a relic species from an earlier time when the area was much wetter. Nowadays, they spend over 90% of their time underground to avoid the heat and hibernate in the winter. They take 15-20 years to reach sexual maturity and can live to be more than 80. Breeding occurs in the Spring when they emerge to eat plants brought by seasonal rains. The Desert Tortoise is an endangered species, under constant threat from a wide range of human activities.

Palmer's Penstemon
(*Penstemon palmeri*)

While journeying in the desert, I often pulled over suddenly to check out something, but I was especially excited about this showy thing because I only saw it in one small area of the Mojave National Preserve.

I was disappointed when I learned its name. Europeans often name plants, animals and geographical features after people, frequently people who never saw the subject. Other cultures give names to describe appearance, function or some understanding of a deeper essence, which strikes me as not only more practical but less egotistical.

In the case of this plant, the honored individual did at least have a direct relationship. Edward Palmer (1829-1911), a US botanist and archeologist, collected plant specimens for the Smithsonian, the USDA and other institutions. Impessively, he pressed and dried over 100,000 samples in his career. About 200 species are named after him.

Palmer was also an early ethnobotanist in the US and wrote, "Food Products of the North American Indians" (1871), one of the first works of its kind. Though his technical descriptions are detailed, his tone toward Native Americans is patronizing, which makes me wonder how much he missed.

Facing page:
Bush Beardtongue
(*Keckiella antirrhinoides*)

Also known as Snapdragon Penstemon and Yellow Keckiella. Named for David Daniels Keck (1903-1995), an American botanist; "antirrhinoides" is Greek for "like a nose," which describes the flower's shape. The origin of the common name, "Beardtongue," should be obvious.

Following pages:
Desert Sand-Verbena (*Abronia villosa*)
Annual Wire Lettuce (*Stephanomeria exigua*)

Wallace's Woolly Sunflower
(*Eriophyllum wallacei*)

Acton's Encelia
(*Encelia actoni*)

Kangaroo Rat
(*Dipodomys merriami*)

I was quite thrilled to meet this extraordinary creature whom I'd seen in books but never in real life. I invited the encounter, having scattered sunflower seeds by the fire ring behind my truck, imitating the 20th Century biologist, Edmund Jaeger, who did just that in order to attract animals so he could study them. Just after sunset, I heard some scuffling and peered out the back of my truck to see a single Kangaroo Rat picking up the seeds and stuffing them into its cheeks.

After filling its cheeks, it would scamper away, bounding on its over-sized back legs. And it was fast, so fast I could barely follow it. Then, within a minute or so, it would return from a different direction, fill up again, and then take off at yet another compass point.

Its movements were quite unusual, and Jaeger describes them well:

His usual quiet manner of locomotion when feeding was a kind of scooting foward with body close to the earth and with foot movements so nearly invisible that he appeared for all the world like some mechanical toy moving forward on hidden wheels.

On following nights, it was joined by others. Then the entertainment really started! Kangaroo Rats are quite competitive around food and frequently squabble. They growled, chased each other in circles, and jumped straight up to meet in mid-air, where they kicked and clawed each other. Sometimes they would rise up on their hind legs and box with their tiny fore-legs. I laughed out loud!

They were not very shy. As long as I avoided quick movements, I could get quite close to them while I took photos, lying flat on my belly. If a shift of my hand or swivel of the camera scared them off, they would scamper back in less than a minute. A few times, they even jumped onto my prone body when scattering from their scuffles and were so lightweight I could barely feel them.

A couple weeks later, as I prepared to leave this campsite, I felt a tinge of melancholy, not knowing if I would ever see another Kangaroo Rat again anywhere else. Life, after all, is full of forks in the road, with meetings and partings that we can't predict. So then, as now, I tried to appreciate the sadness as much as the joy.

A baby Kangaroo Rat

Sunset in the village of Joshua Tree

Sources: Books

Jaeger, Edmund C. **Desert Wild Flowers, Revised Edition**. Stanford, California: Stanford University Press, 1969.

Jaeger, Edmund C. **Our Desert Neighbors**. Stanford, California: Stanford University Press, 1950.

MacKay, Pam. **Mojave Desert Wildflowers: A Field Guide to Wildflowers, Trees, and Shrubs of the Mojave Desert, Including the Mojave National Preserve, Death Valley National Park, and Joshua Tree National Park**. Guilford, Connecticut: The Globe Pequot Press, 2003.

Moerman, Daniel E. **Native American Ethnobotany**. Portland, Oregon: Timber Press, 1988.

Munz, Philip A. (edited by Diane L. Renshaw & Phyllis M. Faber). **Introduction to California Desert Wildflowers**. Berkeley, California: University of California Press, 2004.

Sonnenblume, Kollibri terre. **Wildflowers of Joshua Tree Country**. Portland, Oregon: Macska Moksha Press, 2015.

Taylor, Ronald J. **Desert Wildflowers of North America**. Missoula, Montana: Mountain Press Publishing Company, 1998.

Sources: Websites

Bug Guide: bugguide.net
Butterflies and Moths of North America: butterfliesandmoths.org
CalFlora: calflora.org
California Plant Names: Latin and Greek Meanings and Derivations - A Dictionary of Botanical and Biographical Etymology Compiled by Michael L. Charters: www.calflora.net/botanicalnames/
CalPhotos: calphotos.berkeley.edu
Digital Desert: digital-desert.com
The Jepson Herbaria, University of California, Berkeley: ucjeps.berkeley.edu
Wikipedia: wikipedia.org

Also of great value for initial crowd-sourced identification of both flora and fauna were the following Facebook groups: Butterfly Enthusiast, California Native Plant Society, Insect Identification, Mothing & Moth Watching, and Reptile & Amphibian Identification.

Geometrid Moth (*Glaucina erroraria*)

Acknowledgements

I express sincere gratitude to the following, who made this project possible: Deva for providing camera equipment and other material support, Elaine Close for a place to put it together, Nikki Hill for botanizing and good company, Laurie Troeger Milliard for editing and proof-reading, Rachael L. McIntosh for essential aesthetic assistance, and Jan Stolen for financial backing. Thanks, too, to the Leonard brothers, Michael & JP, for their hospitality in Joshua Tree.

Technical Details

Cameras used:
Nikon Powershot SX110 IS in 2015
Fujifilm X30 in 2016

Hardware/OS:
Dell Latitude laptop (2012) set up with Linux Mint 17.1 'Rebecca' from FreeGeek in Portland, OR, USA: freegeek.org

Software (all open-source):
GIMP 2.8 for color correction, cropping, etc.
Gwenview 4.14.0 pre, for photo previewing and juxtaposition
Scribus 1.4.3.svn for page layout
gedit 2.30.4 for text composition

Fonts:
Ubuntu Regular and **Bold** for body text
Special Elite Regular for titles
Century Schoolbook L Italic for botanical names and quotations
Ubuntu Condensed Regular for publication information
Silk RemingtonSBold Semi-Bold for titles on front cover

www.ingramcontent.com/pod-product-compliance
Lightning Source LLC
Chambersburg PA
CBHW060804270326
41927CB00002B/47